PEARL HARBOR

Essential Events

PEARL HARBOR

BY SUSAN E. HAMEN

Content Consultant
Gregory J. W. Urwin, PhD
Professor of History
Temple University

ABDO
Publishing Company

CREDITS

Published by ABDO Publishing Company, 8000 West 78th Street, Edina, Minnesota 55439. Copyright © 2009 by Abdo Consulting Group, Inc. International copyrights reserved in all countries. No part of this book may be reproduced in any form without written permission from the publisher. The Essential Library™ is a trademark and logo of ABDO Publishing Company.

Printed in the United States.

Editor: Paula Lewis
Copy Editor: Amy Van Zee
Interior Design and Production: Ryan Haugen
Cover Design: Nicole Brecke

Library of Congress Cataloging-in-Publication Data
Hamen, Susan E.
  Pearl Harbor / by Susan E. Hamen.
    p. cm. — (Essential events)
  Includes bibliographical references and index.
  ISBN 978-1-60453-517-4
  1. Pearl Harbor (Hawaii), Attack on, 1941—Juvenile literature. I.
Title.

  D767.92.H34 2009
  940.54'26693—dc22

                              2008033103

TABLE OF CONTENTS

Beach on Oahu, Hawaii

DECEMBER 6, 1941

The evening of December 6, 1941, passed as any other Saturday night on the island of Oahu in the U.S. territory of Hawaii. Hawaiian music could be heard from jukeboxes and radios. The waters of the Pacific Ocean lapped at white sand beaches. Thousands of people enjoyed an island paradise.

The U.S. Naval and Army bases at Pearl Harbor on the island of Oahu were home to 70,000 U.S. sailors and soldiers. Pearl Harbor was the navy's most important base. President Franklin D. Roosevelt had moved the Pacific Fleet to Pearl Harbor in the spring of 1940. The harbor on the southern coast of Oahu was in a bay that was 10 miles (16 km) wide. With its narrow approach, it was an easy harbor to protect. Ford Island was positioned in the middle of the harbor and was home to the naval air base. The battleships were moored in an area called Battleship Row.

Fleet Headquarters, Hickam Field Army Air Base, and the hospital were located southeast of Ford Island. Oahu had two additional airfields: Ewa Mooring Mast Field and Wheeler Field. Ewa was across from Hickam, and Wheeler was north of Pearl Harbor.

Despite the blue water of the Pacific Ocean, the warm sands of nearby Waikiki Beach, and the

Commanders

In February of 1941, President Roosevelt named two new commanders to serve in Hawaii. Lieutenant General Walter C. Short was appointed the commanding general of the Hawaiian Department. Admiral Husband E. Kimmel was named the commander in chief of the U.S. Pacific Fleet.

hospitable nature of the Hawaiians, duty at Pearl Harbor was not a dream assignment. Approximately 100 ships were stationed at Pearl Harbor. The men aboard the ships spent their days practicing drills and making routine patrols. Many service personnel considered the base cramped and the housing insufficient.

That evening, military personnel on shore leave enjoyed the restaurants and bars. Some watched a Clark Gable movie at the theater at Hickam Airfield, home of the Hawaiian Air Force. Others

Pearl Harbor

Pearl Harbor, located on the southern end of Hawaii's island of Oahu, is a natural harbor. Because of the pearl oysters in the harbor's waters, native Hawaiians named the harbor *Wai Momi*, which means "waters of pearl."

In 1778, the Hawaiian Islands were discovered by English explorer Captain James Cook. The islands soon became a trading stop. In 1887, the United States and the Hawaiian Kingdom entered into an agreement. The United States was allowed exclusive rights to Pearl Harbor in exchange for allowing Hawaiian sugar to be exported to the United States tax free. Pearl Harbor was used as a port to refuel and repair U.S. ships in the Pacific Ocean.

In 1908, Congress approved plans to create a naval base at Pearl Harbor. In 1910, the United States began dredging the channel at Pearl Harbor to allow larger navy ships to enter. By 1914, Pearl Harbor was home to U.S. Marines and Army personnel. In 1917, Ford Island, which is in the middle of Pearl Harbor, was purchased for use as a joint army and navy base. As Japan's military threat grew greater, the United States increased the number of ships stationed at Pearl Harbor to increase its military presence in the Pacific.

opted for a quiet evening, writing letters and
listening to Hawaiian music on the radio.

All eight battleships stationed at Pearl Harbor
were in port that night, and parties were held
to entertain officers and their wives or dates.
Lieutenant General Walter C. Short, commanding
general of the Hawaiian Department, attended a
benefit show with his wife at nearby Schofield. As
they drove back later that night, he saw the lights of
the ships moored at Pearl Harbor and commented,
"Isn't that a beautiful sight? And what a target they
would make."[1]

A SECRET MISSION

As the soldiers and sailors enjoyed their evening,
six Japanese aircraft carriers moved east through the
Pacific Ocean toward Oahu. Led by Vice Admiral
Chuichi Nagumo, the Japanese planned to execute a
surprise air attack on the naval base at Pearl Harbor.
The mission was top secret. Japan hoped to catch the
U.S. Navy unaware and cripple its strength in the
Pacific.

With three cruisers, two battleships, nine
destroyers, and numerous supply ships surrounding
the six aircraft carriers, the Japanese armada

consisted of 32 vessels. The six carriers—*Akagi, Hiryu, Kaga, Shokaku, Soryu,* and *Zuikaku*—carried as many as 350 planes. Aboard the *Akagi,* Commander Mitsuo Fuchida and his men understood the importance of maintaining secrecy and the element of surprise. The ships traveled north of commercial shipping lanes to avoid being spotted. The attack force was under strict orders to sink any ships it encountered, regardless of nationality. Radio silence was enforced at all times, and no radio messages were sent out. The fleet refueled twice at sea on its way to Hawaii, a difficult and dangerous procedure in rough water.

Approximately 360 miles (580 km) to the south of Oahu, five Japanese submarines closed in on the island. Each submarine—or "mother" sub, as they were called—carried a miniature submarine. These were called midgets. The submarines lay in wait for their part in the surprise attack.

Broken Silence

The next morning, Sunday, December 7, 1941, was the easiest day of the week for those stationed in Oahu. Marines and sailors gathered for a game of softball. Sailors onboard the USS *Nevada* prepared for a tennis tournament, while the band prepared to play the national anthem for the hoisting of the flag. People met on the beach for morning chapel. It promised to be another day in paradise.

But aboard the *Akagi*, Commander Fuchida was up before the sun rose. Dressed in his flight suit, he would join the other pilots on the mission to Pearl Harbor. Far below the flight deck of the aircraft carrier, strong winds caused whitecaps and sprayed the pilots with salt water. Crewmen on deck held tight to the airplanes so they would not be tossed overboard. As the ships rolled on the turbulent waters, Fuchida knew the conditions for takeoff were dangerous for his pilots. Had this been a practice maneuver, it would have been cancelled. Still, they proceeded. Japan could not afford to lose its one chance at a surprise attack on the U.S. Pacific Fleet. Even if some pilots crashed into the sea at takeoff, the mission would proceed. Two seaplanes had left at 5:30 a.m. to scout the route and confirm whether the coast was clear.

The pilots climbed into their cockpits and started their engines.

Names

The U.S. aircraft carriers were named after U.S. battles and famous former navy ships (*Enterprise*, *Lexington*, and *Saratoga*). The names of Japan's aircraft carriers were more creative. Japanese aircraft carriers that were part of the attack on Pearl Harbor included: *Akagi* (Red Castle), *Kaga* (Increased Joy), *Shokaku* (Happy Crane), *Zuikaku* (Lucky Crane), *Hiryu* (Flying Dragon), and *Soryu* (Green Dragon).

None of the men had a parachute—they were expected to go down with their planes if they were hit. The Japanese pilots accepted this and considered it an honor to die for their country.

Fuchida climbed into his bomber. Its red and yellow stripe around the tail designated it as the flight leader's aircraft. The crew chief handed him a gift from the maintenance crews—a *hashamaki*, the traditional Japanese warrior's headband. Fuchida tied the *hashamaki* around his forehead and saluted his men.

The carriers turned into the wind and increased their speed. At 6:00 a.m., 183 planes began taking off from the six aircraft carriers. They circled the ships, fell into formation, and headed toward Pearl Harbor. Radio waves from a Honolulu radio station guided them toward their target. Their mission was simple: inflict as much destruction as possible on the ships stationed at Pearl Harbor. Their goal was to cripple the U.S. Pacific Fleet.

Tradition

As the Japanese pilots prepared for battle, each man put on a special belt called a *senninbari*. These "thousand-stitch" belts were traditional garments, and with every stitch, the sewer said a prayer for the protection of the wearer. The pilots then gathered around portable Shinto shrines. They drank *sake* and offered up prayers for a successful mission. Before leaving, the men enjoyed *sekihan,* a traditional dish of red beans and rice, which was usually served for special celebrations.

A 1945 photo of Japan's flight commander Mitsuo Fuchida

Franklin Roosevelt (left) and Winston Churchill (right) seated on a British battleship on August 14, 1941, surrounded by army and naval leaders

A WORLD AT WAR

*I*n the late 1930s, the United States was pulling itself out of the Great Depression and living with the devastating droughts of the Dust Bowl. President Franklin Delano Roosevelt's New Deal programs had offered financial relief and aid for many U.S. citizens. By 1941, the country was on a slow path to recovery.

War had been raging in Europe since September 1939. World War II pitted Germany and Italy against France and Great Britain. France had fallen to Adolf Hitler's German troops in June 1940. Soon, Great Britain was the only country in Europe that was able to fend off a German invasion. Germany had already taken over Poland, Denmark, and Norway. Winston Churchill, Great Britain's prime minister, looked for help from the United States. Although President Roosevelt sent aid to Great Britain in the form of war materials through the Lend-Lease Act, the United States was not eager to become involved with a war that leaders believed did not concern them. That would all change on December 7, 1941, when Japan would force the United States to take action.

JAPANESE AGGRESSION

Two days before declaring war against Russia in February 1904, Japan launched a surprise attack against the Russians. This marked the beginning of the Russo-Japanese War. When Japan took over Korea in 1910, it gained even more land. As a result of these conquests, Japan gained some of the natural resources it was seeking. However, it was far from satisfied.

Japan struggled economically after World War I. With very few natural resources, Japan had to rely on other countries for imports of items such as iron, oil, natural gas, and rubber. Neighboring Asian countries had these natural resources in abundance; however, the European powers controlled most of these countries. Resources from the nearby Asian countries were shipped to Great Britain, France, and Holland for their use. The Europeans, not the Asians, benefited from Asian resources.

In addition to a lack of resources, Japan was becoming overpopulated and losing farmland. Japanese leaders felt the only solution was to gain more land rich in natural resources for the Japanese empire.

By the 1920s, Japan was eager to make itself the greatest power in Asia. With the Depression of the 1930s, which affected most of the world, Japanese leaders had the opportunity they needed to proceed with their plan for dominance. The Japanese set out to rid Asia of European rule with the battle cry, "Asia for Asians!" While their plan may have appeared to be in the best interest of their fellow Asians, Japan knew if it could free Asia of European rule, it would stand a better chance of taking over neighboring lands.

The young men of the Imperial Japanese Army understood the circumstances their nation faced. They had grown up in poverty and were fiercely loyal to Emperor Hirohito, who came to power in 1926. They believed Hirohito embodied the spirit of the Japanese people. In an endeavor to restore honor to their nation, a group of

Hirohito

Emperor Hirohito was born Michinomiya Hirohito on April 29, 1901. He reigned as emperor of Japan from 1926 until his death on January 7, 1989. He was the longest-reigning monarch in the history of Japan. The Japanese refer to his reign as *Showa*, or "Enlightened Peace."

Japanese Army officers formed a political party with the goal of establishing Japan as a great world power. The officers of the Imperial Japanese Army felt the United States and other Western countries were in Japan's way of becoming a great nation. Japanese politicians who were on good terms with the United States were assassinated, and international relations between the two countries deteriorated further.

In September 1931, the Imperial Japanese Army invaded and seized Manchuria in northern China. In 1937, Japan began a campaign to take over the rest of China. Japanese soldiers bombed Chinese cities and killed men, women, and children in their path, without mercy. One such incident became known as "The Rape of Nanking." The Imperial Japanese Army also released rats that carried deadly bacteria and infected defenseless civilians. In 1940 and 1941, Japan occupied the French colony of French Indochina (which later became the countries of Vietnam, Laos, and Cambodia) to gain access to their resources of oil and tin. There was an outcry from the powers of the world. Japan was accused of heinous acts that threatened world peace.

THE UNITED STATES RESPONDS

In response to Japan's aggression against China, the United States sent millions of dollars in relief aid to China. Officials in Washington DC began fortifying the Pacific territories against Japanese invasion. On July 25, 1940, in an attempt to force Japan to stop its acts of aggression, President Roosevelt ordered an embargo on aviation fuel and other raw material exports to Japan. Additionally, all Japanese assets in the United States were frozen. This meant that Japan did not have the resources or the financial power its military needed to continue its invasions.

Two months later, on September 27, 1940, Japan entered into a pact with Germany and Italy—the Tripartite Pact—forming the Axis Alliance. The Axis powers would work together to achieve their military and economic goals. By signing the Tripartite Pact, Japan was inching closer to a war with the United States. Japan's plans to continue with aggressive military tactics were in place.

With Japan's taking over of Indochina in July 1941, President Roosevelt added oil to the embargo list.

Lend-Lease Act

In June of 1940, Italy entered World War II. It allied with Germany against Great Britain and France. It was evident that France would soon fall. In an address on June 10, 1940, President Roosevelt declared that U.S. resources and war materials would be sent to Great Britain and France to aid in the fight. By U.S. law, the war materials had to be paid for in cash. By December, Great Britain had ordered more U.S. munitions and materials than it would ever be able to repay.

On December 8, 1940, President Roosevelt proposed the idea of a lend-lease agreement to the U.S. Congress. The United States would provide war materials, food, clothing, services, and information to any country whose defense was vital to the United States. In exchange, the president could accept repayment "in kind or property, or any other direct or indirect benefit which the President deems satisfactory."[1] Congress passed the Lend-Lease Act in March 1941. This gave President Roosevelt an enormous amount of power. By November of 1941, approximately $13 billion had been granted to Great Britain, China, and the Soviet Union in aircraft, tanks, and vital supplies. By the end of the war, more than $49 billion in aid had been dispersed, most of which ended up being outright gifts.

The Panama Canal also was closed to the Japanese. Japan viewed the U.S. Naval Fleet at Pearl Harbor as the only power that could stop their takeover of the Pacific nations.

A Third Term

After two terms as president, Franklin Roosevelt was looking forward to retirement. However, Europe was in a crisis as Hitler was overtaking Europe and Japan was continuing its aggressive stance. Roosevelt understood the need for a strong U.S. leader with experience.

Roosevelt addressed the nation on July 19, 1940, accepting the nomination to run for a third term: "I have asked myself whether I have the right, as Commander-in-Chief of the Army and Navy, to call on men and women to serve their country . . . and, at the same time, decline to serve my country in my own personal capacity, if I am called upon to do so by the people of my country."[2]

President Franklin Roosevelt in the White House in 1937

Japan's Admiral Yamamoto planned the attack on Pearl Harbor in 1941.

Plans to Attack

Admiral Isoroku Yamamoto, commander in chief of the Japanese Combined Fleet, was strongly against a union with the Axis powers. Highly respected by his colleagues, Yamamoto had risen through the ranks of the

Imperial Japanese Navy. He had studied in the United States at Harvard University, where he learned a great deal about Western culture. In 1921, Yamamoto, the future admiral, was one of a group of Japanese advisers who attended the Washington Naval Conference by invitation of President Warren G. Harding. The nations that attended shared interests in the Far East. Their goal was to come to an agreement on ways to decrease military buildup in the Pacific.

In 1924, Yamamoto was stationed in Kasumigaura, northeast of Tokyo. He was made executive officer of the Japanese navy flight school. His students went through an intense training program and were expected to adhere to high standards of discipline. The result was a highly efficient base. Yamamoto furthered his knowledge about the United States when he served as a naval attaché in Washington DC from 1925 to 1928.

Yamamoto believed that the future success of the Japanese military relied upon aircraft carriers that would allow for air strikes during battle. But not everyone agreed with him. The Japanese began constructing two new super-battleships, the *Yamoto* and the *Musashi*. Yamamoto considered this a waste of naval resources. By the end of 1936, Yamamoto was given the chance to pursue his career when he was appointed Vice Navy Minister of the Imperial Japanese Navy.

PLANNING A SURPRISE ATTACK

In 1940, Admiral Yamamoto began formulating a plan to attack Pearl Harbor, the stronghold of the U.S. Naval Fleet. Although Yamamoto did not agree with his country entering into the Tripartite Pact with Germany and Italy, he was unfailingly loyal to his country.

Imperial Navy

The Imperial Japanese Navy adhered to a belief system known as *Bushido*. This means "Way of the Warrior." It is the code of the samurai that began seven centuries earlier. By the mid-1800s, Bushido was the basis of ethical training for Japan. The emperor was revered with complete loyalty and self-sacrifice by his subjects. Bushido includes the:

> . . . ideals of martial spirit, including athletic and military skills as well as fearlessness toward the enemy in battle. . . . But the supreme obligation of the samurai was to his lord. . .[1]

The adherence to the code contributed to the rise of civilian morale in Japan. Japanese nationalism was strong, and the people felt an unquestionable reverence for the emperor.

The Japanese pilots carried out their mission with honor, courage, and loyalty. They were prepared for self-sacrifice. According to the code, they were expected to commit suicide instead of being taken prisoner, which would bring disgrace to the man's family. Japanese prisoners of war often tried to commit suicide, and many changed their names so their parents would think they were dead. This would save their parents from the disgrace of a son held captive.

He wrote to Prime Minister Prince Fumimaro Konoye, "Now that the situation has come to this pass, I hope you will endeavor to avoid a Japanese-American war."[2]

Yamamoto strongly believed that if Japan had any chance against a giant such as the United States, the Japanese had to strike first. Japan had to catch the United States off guard and cripple the U.S. Pacific Fleet. By leaving the U.S. Navy scrambling to recover, Japan would be free to push ahead into other parts of the Pacific.

He wrote to Vice Admiral Koshiro Oikawa, explaining that "the time had come for the Navy to devote itself seriously to war preparations."[3] He asked that he be considered for commanding the mission "so that I may personally command that attack force."[4] Yamamoto supported the suggestion of an attack against Pearl Harbor, explaining that the Imperial Navy should "fiercely attack and destroy the U.S. main fleet at the outset of the war, so that the morale of the U.S. Navy and her people [will] sink to the extent that it could not be recovered."[5]

Japan's goal was to avoid a long, drawn-out war with the United States, and Yamamoto was the man chosen to plan the attack. As commander of

Japan's Combined Fleet, Admiral Yamamoto's plan included launching a surprise air raid against the U.S. Pacific Fleet. Yamamoto's goal was to take out as many of the U.S. battleships—the perceived backbone of the U.S. Navy—as possible. Battleships were floating fortresses, armed with huge guns, and able to withstand a pounding from the enemy with their thick armor. A navy's strength was measured by its battleships.

Doubts

Although Admiral Yamamoto planned the attack on Pearl Harbor, he had serious doubts about Japan's ability to eventually defeat the United States. He wrote in a letter, "Should hostilities break out between Japan and the United States, it would not be enough that we take Guam and the Philippines, nor even Hawaii and San Francisco. To make victory certain, we would have to march into Washington and dictate the terms of peace in the White House. I wonder if our politicians . . . have confidence as to the final outcome and are prepared to make the necessary sacrifices."[6]

TRAINING FOR THE MISSION

Yamamoto began training the air crews on his aircraft carriers in the spring of 1941. The men practiced taking off from the decks of the carriers in rough waters. They learned to refuel their ships at sea, which would be necessary on their long journey from Japan. Pilots practiced the low altitude attack angles that would be used over the harbor. In October, Yamamoto received final approval from the Imperial Japanese Navy to execute his plan. Vice Admiral

Chuichi Nagumo was placed in command of the special task force.

December 8, 1941, was selected for the attack—December 7 in Hawaii's time zone. The Japanese called this "X-Day." They specifically chose it because it was a Sunday. They knew from their spies in Hawaii that the majority of the U.S. Navy's ships would be in port and could be destroyed.

Yamamoto's plan would work only if Japan could take the U.S. Navy by surprise. Vice Admiral Chuichi Nagumo would be able to call off the attack if he felt his strike force had lost the element of surprise. The decision would be up to him after December 6. Until that day, Japanese naval high command could call off the mission.

No Hope of Avoiding War

On November 26, negotiations with Japanese ambassadors in Washington DC failed. It was quite clear to President Roosevelt that relations with Japan were disintegrating. That same day, Vice

Spies in Hawaii

The Japanese Navy sent Lieutenant Takeo Yoshikawa, a specially trained spy, to Hawaii to discover valuable information that would be needed to plan the surprise attack. Under the alias Tadashi Morimura, the 29-year-old spy arrived in Honolulu in March 1941. He then "set out to amass information on a huge scale. He . . . found it easy to spy on the Army and Navy bases, to identify the ships in harbor, and to record their movements and habits—including the low level of activity in the fleet on the weekends."[7]

Admiral Nagumo ordered 23 warships and 8 oil tankers to prepare for departure for Hawaii.

Japan did not formally declare war against the United States. On December 1, 1941, while Washington officials still believed that peace talks to avoid war were under way, Japan made the decision to proceed with the attack against Pearl Harbor.

On December 2, 1941, Admiral Husband E. Kimmel, Commander in Chief of the U.S. Pacific Fleet, received a report from his intelligence officer. The United States was expecting aggressive action from Japan against the Philippines, Thailand, or Borneo. The message Admiral Kimmel received from his immediate commander, Admiral Harold R. Stark, described the worsening relations between the United States and Japan as a "war warning."

Code Words

Mentioned in the code words to proceed with the mission, Mount Niitaka was the tallest peak in the Empire of Japan. The phrase "'Climb Mount Niitaka' signified that Japan was about to scale the most formidable symbolic mountain in its history."[9]

However, officials in Washington did not expect an attack on Pearl Harbor. They believed an attack would be farther south in the Pacific.

That same day, Admiral Yamamoto radioed Nagumo's strike force with the code words that meant to proceed with the mission: "Climb Mount Niitaka."[8]

Japanese Vice Admiral Nagumo commanded the
Pearl Harbor Task Force.

A photograph taken by a Japanese photographer minutes before the attack on Pearl Harbor shows how closely U.S. ships were positioned.

INTO THE WAR

Admiral Yamamoto's attack on Pearl Harbor utilized three different types of aircraft. The first wave of planes to leave the flight decks on the morning of December 7, 1941, consisted of 43 Mitsubishi A6M2s, or "Zeros."

Each fighter plane carried only a pilot and was armed with machine guns and one 132-pound (60-kg) cannon under each wing. With a top speed of 340 miles per hour (547 km/h), it was the job of the Zeros to protect the bombers by shooting down enemy aircraft before they could inflict any damage.

After the Zeros were airborne, the "Kates," 49 Nakajima B5N2 attack bombers, took off. Each Kate had a pilot, a navigator-bomber, and a radioman. A Kate could carry a 1,764-pound (800-kg) armor-piercing torpedo or a 1-ton (0.9-tonne) bomb. The B5N2 bombers would descend to 100 feet (30 m) above the water, fly directly at the target ship, and drop the torpedo. Engines on the torpedo would propel it through the water and straight to its target.

Nicknamed the "Val," 54 of the two-man crew Aichi D3A1

Torpedo Aircraft

Around 1910, the navies of several different countries began experimenting with launching torpedoes from low-flying airplanes. On August 12, 1915, the first effective use of a torpedo launched from a British seaplane destroyed a Turkish vessel. By World War II, the torpedo airplane would play a large role in combat. Torpedo aircraft were utilized by the Japanese in the attack against Pearl Harbor. The United States would later use torpedo aircraft in its 1942 victory at Midway Island.

Japanese pilots walked to their bombers on the flight deck of their aircraft carrier shortly before attacking Pearl Harbor.

dive-bombers took to the air. The pilot sat in the front. The gunner sat behind him and faced the opposite direction. The gunner manned one machine gun in the tail, while the pilot controlled the two machine guns on the nose of the plane. The Val was equipped to carry one 550-pound (250-kg) bomb under the fuselage or two 132-pound (60-kg) bombs—one under each wing. The D3A1 pilots would dive straight down at a target and release a bomb. They would then quickly pull up to avoid the explosion. Finally, 40 more Kates took off. Each carried specially modified torpedoes.

Midget Submarines Wait for Battle

Below the surface of the ocean, miniature submarines, called midgets, lay in wait at Pearl Harbor. Specially designed and built by the Japanese, each midget carried a two-man crew. Approximately 79 feet (24 m) long, each of the five midget submarines carried two torpedoes. The midget submarines were launched from mother submarines the night before the attack and entered Pearl Harbor unnoticed. They would serve as another surprise tactic against the U.S. Navy.

The Japanese military had mixed opinions about the use of the miniature submarines. Many officers felt the midgets would be detected and, therefore, tip off the U.S. Navy that an attack was imminent. They also argued that, should the midgets slip in undetected, they would only inflict minimal damage. Nonetheless, the midgets were deployed. Their mission was to await the air strike and then fire their two torpedoes at any U.S. ships within range. After releasing both torpedoes, each submarine

2 all midget submarine crews would lose their lives carrying out their mission for their country.

Midget Submarines

While the midget submarines were an experimental design, they were advanced for their time. Each battery-powered midget sub was designed to hold two sailors and carry two torpedoes. The subs were approximately 79 feet long (24 m) and approximately 6 feet (2 m) in diameter. Each weighed approximately 46 tons (42 tonnes). Completed only months before the attack on Pearl Harbor, the crew members had very little time to train. The Japanese originally intended that the miniature subs would take down battleships in the high seas. They never fulfilled this purpose.

These subs, knows as type A midget submarines, had design problems. These included difficulty with controls and problems with battery life. Although the Japanese Navy hoped their five midget subs would act as a secret weapon, the subs turned out to be ineffective.

None of the five midget submarines made it back to its mother sub. Three were sunk—one in the harbor and two at the harbor entrance. One ran aground and was captured. The fifth midget sub is still unaccounted for. Periodic searches continue for the missing fifth sub.

Preparation for the midget submarine launch began shortly after midnight on December 7. The five mother submarines were positioned approximately ten miles (16 km) from the mouth of Pearl Harbor. They were able to make out the sounds of jazz music and the lights from Waikiki.

By 3:00 a.m. on the morning of December 7,

1941, four of the five midgets had been launched. One of the five, piloted by Ensign Kazuo Sakamaki and crewed by Seaman Kyoji Inagaki, was left behind to deal with a broken gyroscope. The two had discovered the problem during a last-minute inspection of their midget submarine. Without a properly working gyroscope, they would not be able to navigate underwater. As the other four midget submarines were deployed, the two men stayed behind. They spent the next two hours working on the gyroscope.

A Costly Mistake

At 3:42 a.m., an officer aboard the U.S. minesweeper *Condor* spotted the periscope of a midget sub in the water. An alert was sent to the U.S. destroyer *Ward,* which was patrolling the channel entrance into Pearl Harbor. Unfortunately, the skipper on the *Ward,* Lieutenant William W. Outerbridge, misunderstood the warning and searched for the submarine in the wrong area. Four hours before the attack, the U.S. Navy missed its chance at discovering the planned attack on Pearl Harbor. A midget submarine had been spotted— Japan's worst fear—yet nothing had happened.

And it would not be the last opportunity missed by the United States.

By 5:30 a.m., Sakamaki's midget submarine launched with a broken gyroscope. When his skipper, Lieutenant Commander Hiroshi Hanabusa, asked him if the gyroscope problems would hamper his plans to launch, he replied, "Captain, I am going ahead." They both shouted together, "On to Pearl Harbor!"[1]

First Shots of War

Around 6:30 a.m., the helmsman on the *Ward*, Seaman H. E. Raenbig, spotted something in the water. A black object looked as though it was attached to the towline of the USS *Antares*. Quartermaster H. F. Gearin took a closer look and the two men alerted Lieutenant Junior Grade Oscar Goepner. At first, Gearin and Goepner thought it might be a buoy, but they quickly realized the strange object was more than a simple buoy. It appeared to be a conning tower of a submarine. Goepner shouted for Lieutenant Outerbridge, "Captain, come on the bridge!"[2]

Immediately, the *Ward* began steaming in the direction of the conning tower. The midget submarine was taken down with depth charges, although the U.S. Navy was still unclear where the submarine had come from. Lieutenant Outerbridge sent a radio report at 6:51 a.m., "Depth-bombed sub operating in defensive sea area."[3] In an attempt to get the point across that this was not simply a whale they had mistaken for a sub, Outerbridge sent a follow-up message two minutes later at 6:53 a.m. to the Fourteenth Naval District Headquarters. His message reported, "Attacked, fired on, depth-bombed, and sunk, submarine operating in defensive sea area."[4] The report fell on deaf ears.

Meanwhile, Ensign Sakamaki and Seaman Inagaki attempted to get their midget sub on course. With the gyroscope broken, they used a periscope but were off course. Moving blindly, Sakamaki began to get nervous as 7:00 a.m. approached. They were still a great distance from the mouth of Pearl Harbor.

"Large Number of Planes Coming in from the North"

At the army's Opana radar station, Private Joseph Lockard and Private George Elliott were nearing the end of their 4:00 to 7:00 a.m. shift. The radio station, located on the northern tip of Oahu, had

Radar

At the time of the attack, radar was a relatively new defense tool on the bases. In operation for less than a month, many operators were still learning and practicing their skills.

Radar works by transmitting electromagnetic energy and monitoring the echoes returning from objects or targets. Radar can determine the location, speed, and sometimes even the size and shape of the targets.

In the 1940s, radar was still very new. But its ability to distinguish faraway objects under poor weather conditions, while accurately determining range and distance, set it apart from other sensing devices.

been in operation for only about two weeks. The radio operators spent a great deal of their time training on the equipment, which could pick up planes within 150 miles (241 km).

Around 6:45 a.m., after an uneventful shift at the controls, the men spotted a flicker on the screen. It looked like a few planes coming in from the northeast. They dismissed them as friendly planes and received permission to close up at 6:54 a.m.

At the Shafter Information Center, the hub for all the radio stations, Lieutenant Kermit Tyler was the only officer on duty. This Sunday morning was quiet, with no activity, until he received a call from one of the stations at 6:10 a.m. reporting a sighting of activity. By 6:45 a.m. there was more confirmation of activity 130 miles (209 km) north of Oahu. At 7:00 a.m., all of the men at Shafter left for breakfast, leaving Lieutenant Tyler alone.

At Opana, Privates Lockard and Elliott were officially off duty, but they decided to stay on and do some training. At 7:02 a.m., Lockard began explaining to Elliott what the echoes and blips on the screen meant. He immediately noticed a blip larger than anything he had seen before. Lockard took Elliott's place at the controls and discovered that many planes were heading their way. Elliott quickly calculated the location of the planes. They called Shafter.

Private Joseph McDonald took the call, and Elliott reported, ". . . a large number of planes coming in from the north, three degrees east."[5] McDonald passed the message on to Lieutenant Tyler, who dismissed it.

When McDonald phoned the two privates, Lockard insisted on speaking directly to Lieutenant Tyler. The blips were becoming larger and closing in fast. They calculated that the planes had to be traveling toward them at a speed of at least 180 miles per hour (290 km/h).

Tyler decided they must be B-17s coming in from the mainland. He assured Lockard, "Well, don't worry about it."[6] When Private McDonald asked him about the planes, Tyler responded, "It's nothing."[7]

Tyler was correct in that B-17s were coming in from California. But the 12 planes Lockard and Elliott saw on radar were not those of the U.S. Army Air Forces. Instead, it was a group of planes far larger and certainly not friendly that were definitely moving closer. Had Tyler reported the radio station discovery to his superiors, further investigation may have shown that it was something to worry about.

"At 07:02 I was sitting at the controls while Lockard peered over my shoulder and instructed me on how to detect planes. Suddenly, there appeared the largest blip either of us had ever seen on an oscilloscope. 'What's this?' I asked him. Lockard thought the unit had either malfunctioned or was giving us a false reading. He quickly tested the equipment and determined everything to be working perfectly. We calculated the blip to be a large group of aircraft approaching quickly. . . . I suggested to Lockard that we should notify our Information Center.

"'Don't be crazy!' he laughed. 'Our problem ended at seven o'clock.' However, I was insistent and after a long discussion he said, 'Well, go ahead and send it in if you like.'"[8]

–Private George Elliott, December 7, 1941

*Japanese submarine crew members on a trial run
in December 1941*

This 1961 aerial photograph of Pearl Harbor shows Hickam Air Force Base in the right front.

TORA! TORA! TORA!

As the first wave of Japanese planes neared Oahu, they had a clear view of the island. The Japanese pilots did not use radio communication; they remained silent to keep their presence from being detected. They relied on hand signals to relay messages to one another. Commander Fuchida used Honolulu's radio station signal to check his course.

SURPRISE OR SURPRISE LOST?

Commander Fuchida signaled the order Tenkai, or "Take attack position."[1] At that point, Fuchida had to decide whether or not he felt they had retained the element of surprise. Their mission would be considered either "Surprise" or "Surprise Lost." In the event of Surprise Lost, the dive-bombers and fighters were to attack the airfields and destroy defenses that could counteract the Japanese planes. A Surprise attack meant the dive-bombers would go in last, so the smoke caused by their bombs would not hinder the sight of the pilots. Commander Fuchida would use his signal gun to alert the pilots: once for Surprise and twice for Surprise Lost.

An Opening

As the first wave of Japanese planes flew into Oahu, they were met with dense cloud coverage. Then, as Fuchida later described to the Japanese press, "Through the opening in the clouds, I saw Pearl Harbor, glistening in the sun. 'God must be with us,' I thought. 'It must be God's hand which pulled aside the clouds directly over Pearl Harbor.'"[2]

An undated photo of the USS Arizona with crew members on deck

Fuchida was unsure whether they had been detected, and he heard nothing from the two reconnaissance planes. However, he had a decision to make. The Honolulu radio station was playing music. Fuchida interpreted this as a sign that the U.S. base had no idea the attack was coming; otherwise, it probably would have issued warnings. He also noticed his planes were the only ones in the air. Surely, if the United States had any hint an attack was coming, it would have pilots in the air, prepared to defend Pearl Harbor. At 7:40 a.m., he fired once for Surprise. The flight spread out and prepared for the attack.

Fuchida immediately noticed that the fighter planes were not falling into the proper formation. He assumed they had missed the flare. He waited approximately ten seconds and fired a second shot. Lieutenant Commander Kakuichi Takahashi mistook the second flare as a two-shot Surprise Lost signal and led his dive-bombers toward Ford Island and Hickam Field. The other pilots had no choice but to follow the Surprise Lost plans. The bombs were the first weapons to be used, not torpedoes.

Tora! Tura! Tora!

At 7:49 a.m., Commander Fuchida gave his pilot the attack order to charge. He then instructed his radioman to tap out the order for the other pilots. At 7:53 a.m., Commander Fuchida broke radio silence when he called out, "*Tora! Tora! Tora!*" meaning, "Tiger! Tiger! Tiger!"[3] This was the code word meaning they had caught the U.S. Naval Pacific Fleet by surprise. Their planning and careful preparation had proven a success. The two Japanese admirals aboard the *Akagi* congratulated each other.

Commander Fuchida's pilots broke into separate groups. The torpedo bombers split into two groups of eight planes and sped toward the west side of Pearl Harbor. Two more groups of twelve planes each headed toward Battleship Row where seven battleships were moored along the northeast shore of Ford Island. The *Nevada* and the *Arizona* were the first battleships in the row. A repair ship—the *Vestal*—was stationed alongside the *Arizona*. The *Tennessee* and the *West Virginia* were moored side by side, as well as the *Maryland* and the *Oklahoma*. The *California* was the last battleship in Battleship Row. The *Pennsylvania* was in a nearby dry dock for repair. These eight battleships were the backbone of the U.S. Pacific Fleet.

A Change in Plans

Japanese spies had made careful observations about the locations of the ships and the schedules. As Fuchida flew into range of Pearl Harbor, he noticed there were two less battleships than had been reported that morning by a scout plane. Fuchida's true disappointment lay in the fact that there were no U.S. aircraft carriers stationed at Pearl Harbor on the morning of December 7, 1941. According to Gordon Prange, author of *At Dawn We Slept: The Untold Story of Pearl Harbor*:

> Fuchida fairly ground his teeth in angry frustration as the precise tactical plan he . . . had so painstakingly worked out shattered against that unpredictable element—the human equation. But he soon saw that the order in which they attacked mattered little. The fact of success was assured; the only remaining consideration was its degree.[4]

Two sailors on the pier as the Japanese attack Pearl Harbor

The Japanese pilots had memorized the locations
of the ships, which had been provided by Japanese
spies. Each pilot was given specific targets.

There were approximately 130 vessels in Pearl
Harbor on the morning of December 7, 1941,
in addition to the eight battleships. As many as
eight cruisers, thirty destroyers, and various other
submarines, minelayers, minesweepers, and repair
ships were anchored in the harbor. The three aircraft
carriers were not at Pearl Harbor when the Japanese

Battleship Row

Eight battleships were in Pearl Harbor at the time of the Japanese attack. The ships and their fate are as follows:

- USS *Arizona*: Sunk
- USS *California*: Sunk
- USS *Maryland*: Damaged
- USS *Nevada*: Damaged
- USS *Oklahoma*: Capsized and sunk
- USS *Pennsylvania*: Damaged
- USS *Tennessee*: Damaged
- USS *West Virginia*: Sunk

The *Oklahoma* was stripped of all important war materials and scrapped after the war. The gun turrets, weapons, and other useful equipment were salvaged from the *Arizona* and the *Utah*—a noncombat training ship. Both ships remain at the bottom of the harbor. The other battleships were recovered, rebuilt, and used in battle again.

attacked. Due to bad weather, they had been unable to return to Oahu after their missions. The *Enterprise* had been delivering fighter planes to Wake Island, the *Lexington* had been sent to carry bombers to Midway Island, and the *Saratoga* had been repaired in California.

The fact that these aircraft carriers were not at Pearl Harbor that morning was one of the most fortunate events in World War II for the United States. These ships were spared destruction at Pearl Harbor. In later battles, these aircraft carriers would lead the way in combat at sea for the first time in military history. The *Enterprise* went on to earn the title of most decorated ship of World War II and helped turn the tide of war in the Pacific theater.

The USS Saratoga *had not returned to Oahu*
before the December 7 attack.

The wreckage of U.S. planes on Hickam Airfield on December 7, 1941

THE FIRST WAVE
STRIKES

Lieutenant Commander Kukuichi Takahashi led the dive-bombers. He dropped the first bomb at 7:55 a.m. on Pearl Harbor. Aboard the U.S. minelayer *Oglala*, Rear Admiral William Rhea Furlong noticed bombers flying, but assumed they were U.S. pilots running drills. He saw the bomb drop on the ramp and thought, "What a stupid, careless pilot not to have secured his releasing gear."[1] But as the pilot passed overhead, Furlong noticed the Japanese red rising sun emblem on the sides of the plane. He immediately shouted to his men to prepare to fight. "Japanese! Man your stations!"[2] The *Oglala* immediately sent out the alarm for all ships to defend themselves against an enemy attack.

Lieutenant Commander Logan Ramsey also saw the first bombs explode from the window of the Ford Island Command Center. He raced to the radio room, where he ordered all radiomen to send out the message, "AIR RAID, PEARL HARBOR. THIS IS NOT A DRILL!"[3]

THE FIRST BOMBS DROP

The U.S. cruiser *Raleigh* and the *Utah*, a training ship, were on the west side of Ford Island. Both were torpedoed by the third and fourth groups of Japanese bombers.

Not a Drill

When the attack began, many people did not realize that the planes filling the sky were Japanese and not part of the U.S. military. Many mistook the air raid for a drill. Not until some of the sailors spotted the large red circles on the planes did they know the planes were Japanese.

As the *Utah* began to list, or tilt, after being hit by two torpedoes, the men aboard the *Raleigh* began firing back at the enemy planes. Within five minutes, a pajama-clad Ensign John R. Beardall Jr. had his antiaircraft battery blasting back at the Japanese.

The torpedoes continued to drop. A Japanese torpedo bomber had been gunning for the *Pennsylvania*, but noticing it was in dry dock, he dropped his torpedo on the *Oglala* that was moored next to the light cruiser *Helena*. Both ships were badly damaged by the torpedo that skimmed under the *Oglala* and smashed into the *Helena*. The clock in the engine room of the *Helena* stopped at 7:57 a.m.

The Band Played On

Unfortunately, not all sailors on the ships could clearly see what was happening. Some assumed the army was running drills that had gone a bit too far. Sailors and the marine guard aboard the *Nevada* were lined up in two rows, ready to hoist the U.S. flag, as the band played "The Star-Spangled Banner." At 7:55 a.m., they had five minutes to wait before the 8:00 a.m. playing of morning colors. They noticed low-flying planes diving at the other end of Ford Island. As the minutes ticked by, the band

*The wing of a Japanese bomber
that was shot down over the naval hospital*

leader became worried, but he and his men struck
up the music at precisely 8:00 a.m. A Japanese plane
headed toward them and the rear gunner shot at
the men on deck, miraculously missing all of them.
The band leader hesitated for a brief moment, but
continued directing the band. As the deck of the ship
was strafed all around them, the musicians paused
and then continued with the national anthem.

The flag was the only casualty of the passes by
Japanese planes and was ripped to shreds by the

machine guns as it was hoisted. After the final note of the national anthem was played, the men scurried for cover. Antiaircraft gunners quickly began returning fire. They shot down one Japanese plane before being hit by a torpedo that tore a hole in the side of the ship at 8:03 a.m. Soon, the battleship was targeted by more bombs.

TERROR ON BATTLESHIP ROW

Up and down Battleship Row, the men on the ships began to realize that this was not a drill. Buglers blew the signal for general quarters to alert all crew to report to their stations immediately.

By 8:05 a.m., the *Raleigh* was listing to port. The Japanese continued strafing it. Crew members successfully shot down five enemy airplanes, while struggling to stay afloat. At the same time, crew aboard the repair ship *Vestal* began firing back. The *Vestal* was hit by two bombs—two men were killed and many more were wounded. The battleship *California* was also hit by two torpedoes at 8:05 a.m. Holes were ripped through its side and water flooded in. Men scrambled to keep the boat afloat, but the battleship sunk, nose first, into the mud.

USS Oklahoma

The battleship *Oklahoma* took three torpedoes in the side that allowed water to rush in. As the sleeping sailors on the *Oklahoma* scrambled to quarters to fight back, they had to smash the locks on the chests and magazines holding the ammunition in order to load their antiaircraft and machine guns. Some used hammers and chisels to break into the ammunition, while others struggled to keep their balance as the ship began to list. The firing locks on the antiaircraft guns had been removed in preparation for an inspection the following day. Even with the ammunition, the sailors would not be able to return fire without the firing locks.

A third torpedo struck the ship, and one sailor "had to walk uphill to go to the starboard side."[4] The ship began to lean considerably, and sailors abandoned efforts to fight back in order to evacuate the capsizing ship. Below decks, men sealed off compartments in an effort to stop the water from rushing into the ship but trapped themselves in the process. They thought they could wait for rescuers to come for them, but the bombing continued. The fate of the *Oklahoma* looked bleak. Two more torpedoes hit the ship, for a total of five, as the sailors scrambled overboard. The *Oklahoma* rolled over and sank in the shallow waters of the harbor. The men trapped below deck quickly struggled to get out of the sinking ship. Men became disoriented. The floor was now above them, and the ceiling was below them.

One by one, a group of men, aided by navy chaplain Lieutenant J.G. Father Aloysius Schmitt, squeezed through a porthole to swim to safety. The men were trapped in air pockets as the compartments filled with water. When they tried to pull Schmitt through, it became evident that he was too big to make it through. He insisted they abandon their efforts to save him. He continued to help push more sailors out through the porthole. For his bravery and the sacrifice of his life to help his fellow shipmates, Father Schmitt was awarded the U.S. Navy and Marine Corps Medal posthumously, and a destroyer was named after him in 1943.

The *Oklahoma* lost 429 men stationed on it. Survivors swam for the *Maryland*. Mrs. Earle, Admiral Kimmel's neighbor, later commented,

> *Then slowly, sickeningly, the* Oklahoma *began to roll over on her side. . . . It was awful, for great ships were dying*

before my eyes! Strangely enough, at first I didn't realize that men were dying too.[5]

It took the *Oklahoma* eight minutes to sink after being hit by the first torpedo.

THE BATTLE CONTINUES

As men struggled to evacuate the *Oklahoma*, the *West Virginia* was hit by six or seven torpedoes and two bombs. The ship began to list. Captain Mervyn Bennion, the ship's skipper, and Lieutenant Commander T. T. Beattie, the navigator, agreed to counterflood.

A Wall of Flame and Smoke

When the USS *Arizona* was torpedoed, many men were caught below deck. Some were able to find their way to safety through the fire and smoke. Seaman Second Class George Phraner remembered:

The lights went out and it was pitch black; a thick, acrid smoke filled the magazine locker and the metal walls began to get hot. Somehow we were able to open the hatch and start to make our way up the ladder. I was nauseated by the smell of burning flesh, which turned out to be my own as I climbed up the hot ladder. Getting through that choking kind of smoke was a real ordeal. After a while I began to get weak and light-headed. I could feel myself losing the battle to save my own life. At that moment, I looked up and could see a small point of light through the smoke. It gave me the strength to go on. After what seemed to me like an eternity, I reached the deck gasping and choking. I lay down for a few moments. The warm Hawaiian air filled my lungs and cleared my head. I glanced over to the forward end of the ship to see nothing but a giant wall of flame and smoke.[6]

Last Letter

Captain Franklin Van Valkenburgh, commander of the USS *Arizona*, wrote a letter home to his wife on December 6, telling her "By this time next week, we will be on our way home for Christmas."[7] He died the next day when his ship was bombed as he stood on the ship's bridge.

This corrected the list and prevented capsizing for the moment.

As the crew of the *Arizona* ran to their stations, the battleship was hit with five torpedoes. At approximately 8:08 a.m., an armor-piercing bomb dropped by a Kate hit the *Arizona*. It ignited the ammunition magazine in the front of the ship under the deck and caused a massive explosion as 500 tons (454 tonnes) of ammunition and gunpowder went up in flames. The explosion blew the *Arizona* up and out of the water. Broken in two, it sank into the mud of the shallow harbor. This one devastating explosion killed 1,177 men aboard the *Arizona*—approximately half the deaths of U.S. military personnel on December 7.

Burning wreckage of U.S. Navy battleships bombed by the Japanese

A small boat rescued a crew member from the water; the USS Tennessee *mast is behind the burning USS* West Virginia.

TERROR CONTINUES ON BATTLESHIP ROW

Commander in Chief of the U.S. Pacific Fleet, Admiral Husband E. Kimmel, who was at home at the time of the attack, was notified that the Japanese were bombing Pearl Harbor. While he was on the telephone, a yeoman burst in with the news, "There's a message from the signal tower saying the Japanese are attacking Pearl Harbor and this is no drill."[1]

Admiral Kimmel rushed outside in time to see the battleship *Arizona* "lift out of the water, then sink back down—way down."[2] Kimmel later recalled, ". . . this was not a casual raid by just a few stray planes. The sky was full of the enemy."[3]

The repair ship *Vestal*, moored next to the *Arizona*, had been on fire at the time the last bomb struck the *Arizona*. The explosion of the *Arizona*'s ammunition magazine was so forceful that it sucked the oxygen away from the area around the *Vestal*. This put out the fire on the *Vestal* and knocked approximately 100 sailors overboard.

Oil spilled out from the damaged *Arizona* and caused fire to spread across the surface of the water. Explosions caused by bombs and torpedoes hitting the ships sent fuel oil flying.

A Helpless Situation

Admiral Kimmel could do little more than watch the horror unfold. He stood at the window at his headquarters on the submarine base and witnessed the mighty U.S. Navy ships explode and sink. But it was the knowledge that thousands of his men were suffering and dying that made the helpless situation so hard to bear. As he looked toward Battleship Row, a spent .50 caliber bullet from a machine gun broke through his window and bounced off his chest, leaving the admiral unharmed. As he bent down to pick it up off the floor, he remarked, "It would have been merciful had it killed me."[4]

Kimmel had wanted to lure the Imperial Navy to Wake Island, a small U.S. Naval air station west of Hawaii. If the Japanese were to strike Wake Island, the United States could engage the Japanese in a battle at sea.

Quickly, the waters of Pearl Harbor were ablaze. The *Nevada* began to list and counterflooding measures began. As the flames neared the *Nevada*, the decision was made to get her underway and out to open sea to avoid the fire. It would also keep her from being an easy target for the Japanese. The *Nevada* made for the entrance of the harbor.

CHAOS

Sailors struggled to get the guns firing. Canvas coverings over guns and decks had to be removed. As one sailor fumbled trying to untie knots in the ropes holding down the canvas, a cook quickly cut the lines using a butcher's knife. Men knocked locks off ammunition boxes with fire axes and hammers. Others used saws to break into the boxes.

The *Maryland* and the *Tennessee* were moored between Ford Island and another battleship. They seemed to be the most protected of the battleships. The *Maryland* sat adjacent to the *Oklahoma*, and the *Tennessee* was protected by the *West Virginia*. Nevertheless, the *Maryland* was hit by two bombs, but they caused little damage. The *Tennessee* also took two bombs, but more damage was caused by the pieces of metal and burning oil that rained down from the explosion

Women firefighters during the attack on Pearl Harbor

of the *Arizona*. The crew of the *Tennessee* fought the fires and shot back at the Japanese planes that flew overhead.

The bridge of the *West Virginia* was hit with shrapnel from the bomb that hit the *Tennessee*. Captain Bennion was severely injured in the stomach and lost the use of his legs. His injury would be fatal, but the captain was still conscious. An ensign rushed to his side. With no way of medically helping the captain, the junior officer did what he could to make

Captain Bennion as comfortable as possible. Mess attendant Dorie Miller, a large, muscular man, was brought up to carry the captain to a safer spot, away from the smoke and fire, behind the conning tower. Captain Bennion continued to run the ship until the situation became hopeless. He then ordered his men to leave him and save themselves.

The men who evacuated sinking ships were forced to jump into blazing water. The oil that covered the surface of the water from the wreckage covered the men. Those who jumped overboard and

A Heroic Act of Bravery

African-American Dorie Miller was a mess attendant and the heavyweight boxing champion on the *West Virginia*. When the crew prepared for battle, he found his station wrecked by torpedo damage. He helped carry injured men to safety, including Captain Bennion. Miller also manned an antiaircraft machine gun until ordered to abandon the ship.

Generally, African-American sailors served in the kitchens or as duty guards. Miller had not been trained to operate the antiaircraft weapon, but as he later described,

It wasn't hard. I just pulled the trigger and she worked fine. I had watched the others with these guns. I guess I fired her for about fifteen minutes. I think I got one of those [Japanese] planes. They were diving pretty close to us.[5]

On May 27, 1942, Admiral Chester W. Nimitz presented Miller with the Navy Cross for his acts of heroism in battle. Admiral Nimitz remarked:

This marks the first time in this conflict that such high tribute has been made in the Pacific Fleet to a member of his race and I'm sure that the future will see others similarly honored for brave acts.[6]

surfaced were faced with flames on the water, and thick, black smoke. The clothes of some of the men burned off their bodies. Others choked on the smoke while gasping for air. Rescuers found it difficult to pull some of the men into rescue boats, because their skin was covered in slippery oil. Many men were severely burned as they tried to escape the sinking boats. Nonetheless, sailors scrambled to save their fellow countrymen. Rescue boats darted around the flames, trying to save whoever could be found.

MIDGET SUBMARINES

At 8:17 a.m., one of the midget submarines slipped into the harbor and surfaced. However, the U.S. destroyer *Helm* spotted it as it headed toward the entrance to the harbor and rammed into it at full speed. At 8:36 a.m., the destroyer *Monaghan* spotted another midget submarine. The *Monaghan* rammed, depth charged, and destroyed it immediately. One of the midget submarines disappeared; it still has not been accounted for.

Ensign Kazuo Sakamaki, who had struggled with his gyroscope, did not make it into Pearl Harbor. His midget submarine eventually ran out of battery power and grounded on a coral reef. Both crewmen abandoned the sub and lit the fuse to detonate explosive charges to keep the small submarine out of enemy hands.

Petty Officer Inagaki lost his life in the waters of the Pacific, and Sakamaki was found washed ashore. He became the first Japanese prisoner of war taken by the United States. This was considered dishonorable by the Japanese military. Soldiers and sailors were expected to commit suicide before surrendering or being taken captive. Sakamaki's capture was a disgrace in the eyes of his countrymen.

"They gave the word 'abandon ship' and we just practically stepped off on the quarter deck into the water . . . I didn't know how bad I was hurt. And I got out there about 10 feet and I guess I must have passed out. [I] went down in the water and everything was just as peaceful and nice, that it would have been so easy to just let go. And I saw this bright light and something made me come to. And so I got back up to the surface of the water and the oil was a fire all around; the fire was approaching me, wasn't but two feet from me and he reached down and pulled me up out of the water. And that man saved my life."[7]

—Carl M. Carson,
USS Arizona *survivor*

"above and beyond the call of duty"

DORIE MILLER
*Received the Navy Cross
at Pearl Harbor, May 27, 1942*

*Mess Attendant Dorie Miller was awarded the Navy Cross.
He rescued wounded men and shot at Japanese aircraft.*

A sailor runs from burning planes that were bombed by the Japanese.

AIRFIELDS
UNDER ATTACK

attleship Row was in chaos. The U.S. Army, Navy, and Marine Corps airfields were bombed and strafed. After a bomb took out the seaplane ramp on Ford Island, another bomb blew a utility hangar to pieces. The goal of the Japanese was to destroy all the U.S. planes on the ground to retain control of the air over Pearl Harbor and ruin the chance of U.S. pilots fighting back.

KANEOHE BAY

Kaneohe Bay's Naval Air Station was the first U.S. military base to be attacked. Located approximately 12 miles (19 km) northeast of Honolulu, the naval station housed 36 PBY patrol seaplanes and a few other planes. Three of the PBYs were out on patrol when the Japanese arrived.

At 7:48 a.m., Japanese Zeros fanned out and began firing on Kaneohe Bay. Shortly after, the dive-bombers descended upon Kaneohe. The first bomb destroyed the only fire truck at Kaneohe. One of the cooks ran through the pilots' sleeping quarters, waking up the pilots by banging a spoon against a cake pan and yelling, "They is attacking! They is attacking!"[1] Approximately

Comparisons

None of the U.S. airplanes were able to outfight the Japanese Zeros. The Zeros could out-turn and outclimb the U.S. fighters. Soon, however, U.S. pilots would realize the Zero had no armor and no self-sealing gas tanks. The larger caliber cannons on the Zero were less accurate and had less range than the machine guns on the U.S. fighter planes.

400 sailors, officers, and marines stationed at Kaneohe scrambled to fight back.

Commander Harold M. Martin was impressed by his men, stating, "It was remarkable. There was no panic. Everyone went right to work battling back and doing his job."[2] Five pilots piled into a car and arrived at the airplane hangars, dodging machine gun fire from the Zeros. They found all of the planes ablaze. The Japanese Zeros destroyed all but six of the PBY seaplanes. According to medical records, 17 men at Kaneohe were killed.

HICKAM FIELD

At Hickam Field near Ford Island's Battleship Row, the A-20, B-18, and B-17 bombers had been lined up neatly in rows, wingtip to wingtip, to keep them closely guarded and protected from sabotage. However, this made an easy target for the Japanese bombers. Next, the bombers concentrated their attack efforts on the barracks, the mess hall, the base theater, and the fire station.

Many men were still asleep when the assault on Hickam Field began. The barracks housed 3,200 men. It suffered a direct hit in the center, where the mess hall was located, instantly killing 35 men who were eating breakfast. Struggling to fight back, but completely unprepared, the men resorted to desperate measures. Lieutenant Vernon H. Reeves and some friends shot at the Japanese planes with pistols, and one man lugged a machine gun to the top of an airplane hangar where he opened fire against the enemy. Another man mounted a .30-caliber machine gun in the nose of a B-18 and fired at the enemy until the B-18 was on fire.

Zeros fired their machine guns across Hickam Field as they flew incredibly low over the area. Bombs caused buildings to explode across the airfield. The Japanese attack on Hickam Field killed 189 men and injured 303 men.

FRIENDLY FIRE

As Hickam was under attack, the U.S. B-17 bombers from California en route to the Philippines were arriving, led by Major Truman H. Landon. At first, the U.S. bomber pilots thought the Japanese planes were U.S. planes coming out to greet them. Very soon, however, they realized the planes were not friendly. Major Landon and his pilots were at the end of a 14-hour flight and dangerously low on fuel. They had no machine guns on their planes and had only minimal crews in order to save weight. They had no chance of fighting back against the Japanese.

As the U.S. B-17 planes—nicknamed Flying Fortresses—approached Hickam, Japanese Zeros were on their tails. Flying their best to evade enemy fire, the U.S. pilots soon were forced to contend with friendly fire. U.S. military on the ground fired at them, not realizing they were U.S. planes. The pilots landed wherever they could across the island. Japanese Lieutenant Yoshio Shiga was impressed with the B-17s. They could withstand the guns of the Zeros and land safely, seemingly unharmed.

WHEELER FIELD

Rows of P-36A, P-40B, and P-40C fighter aircraft were lined up on the tarmac in front of the hangars at Wheeler Field, in the middle of Oahu. As at Hickam, the planes were easy targets. Japanese dive-bombers (Vals) dropped their bombs and then returned to make strafing runs. Colonel William J. Flood later explained that the planes were so low, "I could see some of the Japanese pilots lean out of their planes and smile as they zoomed by . . . I could even see the gold in their teeth."[3]

Soon, Zeros joined the bombers and together they unleashed heavy destruction on the base. Men on the ground pushed unharmed planes to safety. A few P-36A and P-40 pilots were able to take to the air, where they battled the Japanese in aerial dogfights. U.S. pilots took down ten Japanese planes.

Lieutenants George S. Welch and Kenneth Taylor had spent the night playing poker. As soon as they heard the machine guns, they phoned Haleiwa Field, a grass landing and takeoff strip near Wheeler, to have their P-40s fueled and armed. As they sped to Haleiwa in Taylor's car, they were pursued by a

Fighting in Pajamas

The U.S. pilots were caught unaware, just as the sailors in Pearl Harbor had been. The majority of U.S. planes were either destroyed or damaged, yet some of the pilots were able to get into the air and return fire on the Japanese.

Lieutenant Philip Rasmussen was still in his pajamas when Wheeler Field came under attack. Frantically, he and other pilots scrambled to get their P-36s armed, fueled, and in the air. Finally, Rasmussen was airborne.

He machine-gunned one Japanese plane and dodged another before a Japanese fighter fired on him. His plane sustained a great deal of damage. The hydraulic lines were severed, the rear wheel was shot off, and two cannon shells hit the radio behind his seat. Nonetheless, Rasmussen was able to land without rudder, brakes, or tail wheel.

Rasmussen recalled, "I shakily got out of my plane, walked over to my room and traded my pajamas for a flying suit, then returned to the flight line." A few days later, he checked his plane and "counted some 450 holes."[4]

Japanese dive-bomber. The two young pilots took to the air. Welch was credited with shooting down four dive-bombers and Taylor downed two. They returned to Wheeler for more ammunition. As they took off, a group of Japanese Vals and Zeros headed toward them. Taylor and Welch flew directly into their formation and as Welch recounted, "I shot down one right on Lieutenant Taylor's tail."[5] Each man later received the Distinguished Service Cross for extraordinary heroism.

The Japanese Vals dropped bombs that ripped open the barracks, killing hundreds of men. Wheeler was left with 83 destroyed aircraft.

Ewa Mooring Mast Field

More strafing runs were made by 21 Zeros on Ewa Field, the marine air station west of Pearl Harbor. At least half of the planes stationed there were destroyed. Men rushed from their tents in an attempt to get inside the planes and up in the air. Spilled gasoline burst into flames, and the area was soon ablaze.

Japanese dive-bombers and fighters coming from Wheeler and Hickam arrived 10 to 15 minutes after the initial strike. The pilots targeted buildings and

The wreckage of a Japanese torpedo plane
was brought up from the bottom of Pearl Harbor.

soldiers. One marine bravely stood on the ground
firing at a Zero with a pistol. More marines were
successful in shooting down Zeros using the gun
mount from a scout plane. After the follow-up attack
by Zeros and Vals, 33 of the 47 aircraft on the field
were destroyed. Two aircraft were barely salvageable.

The Japanese attack had been well planned. On
a Sunday morning, many men were still asleep when
the Japanese struck. Because the U.S. planes had
been grouped together, under the order of General

Short, the airmen had little chance of fighting back against the Japanese bombers and fighters. Yet, many U.S. pilots and crewmen displayed valiant courage under fire, and several lost their lives trying desperately to fight back. —

The lower plane is a B-17 bomber (Flying Fortress). The aircraft
parked at Hickam Field were easy targets for the Japanese.

The USS Cassin *and the USS* Downes *destroyers sustained heavy damage in the attack on Pearl Harbor.*

SECOND WAVE OF ATTACKS

With no hope of defensive help from U.S. aircraft, the navy ships experienced mass destruction in Pearl Harbor. After the initial attack of approximately 30 minutes, the first wave of Japanese planes headed back to the carriers. Ten minutes later, the second wave of planes descended on Pearl Harbor. They were looking for ships that had not been destroyed by the first wave. At 8:50 a.m., 52 Kates, 78 Vals, and 27 Zeros flew into Pearl Harbor. U.S. sailors fired back with antiaircraft guns.

The *Pennsylvania* had been mostly ignored during the first wave because it was in dry dock. At 9:07 a.m., it was hit with a bomb that killed 18 men and wounded 30. In nearby dry docks, the *Cassin*, the *Downes*, and the *Shaw* suffered from the second wave of attacks. The first two destroyers caught fire, and after more explosions, the *Cassin* slowly rolled against the *Downes*.

At 9:08 a.m., bombs were dropped on the *Raleigh*. To prevent the ship from capsizing, all top weight was jettisoned, or thrown overboard, while the guns continued to fire back at the enemy planes.

At 9:12 a.m., the *Shaw* was hit. It exploded into a big ball of fire

Free and Clear

The *Nevada* was making its way to the opening of the harbor on the way out to sea. Japanese pilots zeroed in on it. Soon, rounds of machine gun fire hit the *Nevada*. The Japanese hoped to sink the battleship at the mouth of the harbor, blocking any other U.S. ship from leaving Pearl Harbor. Dive-bombers successfully dropped three bombs on the *Nevada* and ripped open the upper deck. The ship's captain, F. W. Scanland, was not on board when the Japanese attacked. But Lieutenant Commander Francis Thomas understood the intent of the Japanese bombers. He ordered the ship to be run aground at Hospital Point to keep the opening to the harbor free and clear.

around 9:30 a.m., sending five-inch (13-cm) shells tumbling nearly half a mile (.8 km) away.

Around 10:00 a.m., the cruiser *St. Louis* headed through the entrance to Pearl Harbor on its way out to sea. A midget submarine fired both its torpedoes but missed the target, and the *St. Louis* returned fire on the sub.

The Onslaught Ends

The second wave of Japanese planes returned to their aircraft carriers at 9:55 a.m. Commander Fuchida hoped to strike a third time to take out repair docks, dry dock facilities, and oil tanks. Vice Admiral Nagumo decided against another strike, fearing the United States now might be prepared to fight back. Fortunately for the United States, the repair shops, dry dock facilities, and oil tanks were left intact, and these would be used to help repair and rebuild the U.S. Pacific Fleet.

The United States lost 2 battleships, 19 sunken or damaged ships, 164 destroyed aircraft, and 159 damaged aircraft. A staggering 2,388 U.S. lives had been lost, including 48 civilians. Another 1,178 people were wounded. The devastating surprise attack on the U.S. Pacific Fleet had lasted two hours.

The USS Shaw exploded after the Japanese bombed it on December 7, 1941.

During this time, the Japanese lost 29 planes, all 5 midget submarines, and less than 100 men.

Aftermath

Doctors and nurses hurried to treat wounded men at the Tripler Hospital. Within the course of two hours, hundreds of men were in need of medical attention for severe burns, wounds from machine gun fire, shrapnel, and other serious injuries.

Injured men were laid out on lawns while hospital staff, soldiers, and sailors rushed to convert mess halls, barracks, and schools into temporary hospitals.

For many of the severely injured, nurses could only give them morphine to lessen their pain. Oahu civilians offered help where they could. Some helped at the hospitals. Others hauled water and helped fight the fires. Others donated blood. Even young people helped where they could. Lieutenant Commander Logan Ramsey's 16-year-old daughter Mary Ann comforted

Japanese Americans

After the attack, the United States responded with suspicion to anyone living in the United States who was of Japanese heritage. Were they loyal to Japan? Did some participate in acts of espionage? The attack left many wary of their Japanese-American neighbors, most of whom were U.S. citizens or legal resident aliens.

On February 19, 1942, President Roosevelt issued Executive Order 9066. This forced more than 120,000 West Coast U.S. citizens of Japanese descent into internment camps in the name of national defense. Surrounded by barbed wire and armed guards, many spent up to four years waiting to be released. Half were children. Inadequate medical care led to the death of several detainees. Others were killed for allegedly resisting orders. For many, the emotional stress had long-lasting effects. Ironically, people of Japanese descent in the Hawaiian territory were not sent to internment camps or deported. Their presence was considered vital to the economic health of the islands.

On August 10, 1988, Congress acknowledged "a grave injustice was done to both citizens and permanent residents of Japanese ancestry by the evacuation, relocation, and internment of civilians during World War II."[1]

those who lay dying outside a marine barracks-turned-hospital.

Servicemen who had not been present at the time of the attack returned to Pearl Harbor and reported to their posts. Sailors pulled injured men out of the water as rescue boats brought boatloads of men to shore for medical attention.

In the harbor, men were still trapped in sunken ships. Trapped sailors used wrenches and hammers to tap against the metal ships to alert rescuers that they were still alive. Not until the next morning were rescuers able to begin cutting into the *Utah* and the *Arizona* to get sailors out. They followed the sounds of the taps made by the trapped men. By Monday afternoon, Electrician's Mate First Class Irvin H. Thesman and others were rescued from the *Oklahoma*. He described the experience, "It was a deep, powerful feeling . . . like being dug up out of your own grave."[2]

As hundreds of men waited to be rescued from pitch-dark sunken ships, sailors worked with torches to free them. However, cutting into the compartments with acetylene torches not only brought water rushing in, but the first two men to be cut out of the *Oklahoma* died when the torch consumed the oxygen in the compartment and asphyxiated the men. The day of the attack, one man was saved from the *Utah* and six from the *Oklahoma* by cutting into the ships. The next day, 24 men were rescued from the *Oklahoma*.

"You lose all track of time. Then we heard some tapping and we figured something was going on. They tapped one-two, one-two. Then we tapped back. . . . We could see a little bit of light. They are cutting away and I am watching the water below us. The water is coming up and they are cutting. I thought the water was going to beat them. . . . Pretty soon they were up above us, and there was a hatch on this one. They yelled down asking if we were in a dry compartment. I told them 'Yeah,' and they said, 'Stand clear.' The door flops open and there's your rescue party. . . . I lost twenty pounds since I didn't have anything to eat or drink for two days we were trapped in the ship."[3]
—*Walter Staff, survivor, USS* Oklahoma

The men trapped in the *Arizona* had no chance. The ship's deck was ablaze with flames so hot that rescuers were unable to get near the ship. It burned for three days. Only 334 men survived of the 1,511 crew members of the *Arizona*. Of the 1,177 men who died on the *Arizona*, only 107 of the 229 bodies recovered in the days following the attack were identified. The remaining sailors were declared "buried at sea" when the U.S. Navy called off efforts to retrieve the victims.

Honolulu Star-Bulletin 1st EXTRA

8 PAGES—HONOLULU, TERRITORY OF HAWAII, U. S. A., SUNDAY, DECEMBER 7, 1941—8 PAGES ★ PRICE

WAR!

OAHU BOMBED BY JAPANESE PLANE

(Associated Press by Transpacific Telephone)

SAN FRANCISCO, Dec. 7.—President Roosevelt announced this morning that Japanese planes attacked Manila and Pearl Harbor

SIX KNOWN DEAD, 21 INJURED, AT EMERGENCY HOSPITAL

Attack Made On Island's Defense Areas

By UNITED PRESS

WASHINGTON, Dec. 7.—Text of a White House announcement detailing the attack on the Hawaiian islands is:

"The Japanese attacked Pearl Harbor from the air and all naval and military activities on the island of Oahu, principal American base in the Hawaiian islands."

Oahu was attacked at 7:55 this morning by Japanese planes.

The Rising Sun, emblem of Japan, was seen on plane wing tips.

Wave after wave of bombers streamed through the clouded morning sky from the southwest and flung their missiles on a city resting in peaceful Sabbath calm.

According to an unconfirmed report received at the governor's office, the Japanese force that attacked Oahu reached island waters aboard two small airplane carriers.

It was also reported that at the governor's office either an attempt had been made to bomb the USS Lexington, or that it had been bombed.

CITY IN UPROAR

Within 10 minutes the city was in an uproar. As bombs fell in many parts of the city, and in defense areas the defenders of the islands went into quick action.

Army intelligence officers at Ft. Shafter announced officially shortly after 9 a. m. the fact that the bombardment by an enemy but long previous army and navy had taken immediate measures in defense.

"Oahu is under a sporadic air raid," the announcement said.

"Civilians are ordered to stay off the streets until further notice."

The army has ordered that all civilians stay off the streets and highways and not use telephones.

ANTIAIRCRAFT GUNS IN ACTION

First indication of the raid came shortly before 8 this morning when antiaircraft guns around Pearl Harbor began sending up a thunderous barrage.

Hundreds See City Bombed

A December 7, 1941, Honolulu newspaper reports the attack on Pearl Harbor.

*Women worked on bomber planes in 1942
to help in the war effort during World War II.*

A NATION RESPONDS

resident Franklin D. Roosevelt and others in Washington DC knew of the attack on Pearl Harbor minutes after it began. Although Washington officials expected Japan to take action in the Pacific, they were not anticipating such a devastating surprise attack on Pearl Harbor. News of the attack spread throughout the nation. Many people were enjoying the Sunday afternoon at home. Radio news broadcasts broke into regular programming to relay the terrible message.

People listened in horror and anger to the news of the devastation at Pearl Harbor. In a nation deeply saddened, an almost instantaneous sense of U.S. patriotism and determination swept across the country. Any lingering sense of isolationism by U.S. citizens was quickly extinguished by Japan's attack. The country pulled together with "Remember Pearl Harbor!" as the rallying cry.

The next day, Monday, December 8, 1941, President Roosevelt addressed the U.S. Congress, urging them to declare war. His speech was short, but to the point:

Women in the War

The Second World War required the joint efforts of men and women, both at home and abroad. Women served their country in the U.S. Army, Coast Guard, Marines, and Navy Reserve. The occupations these women worked in included cartography, computing, motor mechanics, weather forecasting, parachute packing, mail sorting, and air traffic control. On the home front, millions of women who had never worked outside the home entered the civilian U.S. workforce.

Yesterday, December 7, 1941—a date which will live in infamy—the United States of America was suddenly and deliberately attacked by naval and air forces of the Empire of Japan.

The United States was at peace with that nation, and, at the solicitation of Japan, was still in conversation . . . looking toward the maintenance of peace in the Pacific.

. . . obvious that the attack was deliberately planned many days or even weeks ago. During the intervening time the Japanese Government had deliberately sought to deceive the United States by false statements and expressions of hope for continued peace.

Very many American lives have been lost. In addition American ships have been reported torpedoed on the high seas between San Francisco and Honolulu.

Yesterday, the Japanese government also launched an attack against Malaya.

Last night, Japanese forces attacked Hong Kong.

Last night, Japanese forces attacked Guam.

Last night, Japanese forces attacked the Philippine Islands.

Last night, the Japanese attacked Wake Island.

This morning, the Japanese attacked Midway Island.

. . . The People of the United States . . . understand the implications to the very life and safety of our nation.

. . . As Commander-in-Chief of the Army and Navy I have directed that all measures be taken for our defense.

. . . Hostilities exist. There is no blinking at the fact that our people, our territory, and our interests are in grave danger.

. . . I ask that the Congress declare that since the unprovoked and dastardly attack by Japan on Sunday, December 7, 1941, a state of War has existed between the United States and the Japanese Empire.[1]

Roosevelt's speech lasted only six minutes. In less than one hour, Congress had approved war with a unanimous vote by the Senate and a vote of 388 to 1 in the House of Representatives.

Thousands of young men rushed to enlist. Prior to the Pearl Harbor attack, approximately 1.5 million young men served in the armed forces. As the nation proceeded with a war that would last until 1945, approximately 16 million U.S. citizens served their country in World War II. Approximately 400,000 were women who served in the U.S. military. For the first time in U.S. history, women would be filling positions other than clerks or nurses.

Winston Churchill, the British prime minister, thankfully acknowledged that the United States would be joining the war. His country had been trying to hold the Germans at bay and greatly needed assistance.

RELIEVED OF DUTY

On December 17, 1941, both General Short and Admiral Kimmel were relieved of their commands for failure to be on alert. A full investigation was conducted to determine just how responsible the two men were for failing to defend their posts against the disaster. Many citizens demanded to know how the United States could be caught so badly off guard. But it was soon evident that, despite the destruction and loss of life at Pearl Harbor, the

Cleared

Both Admiral Husband E. Kimmel and General Walter Short were granted retirement almost immediately. The investigation that was conducted in the months following the attack found both men responsible for the disgraceful charge of "dereliction of duty." Kimmel spent his remaining days trying to clear his name. It was not until 2000 that the U.S. Senate passed a resolution stating both men performed their duties "competently and professionally," and that the attacks were "not a result of dereliction of duty."[2]

situation could have been worse. The aircraft carriers were spared, the oil tanks remained intact, and no ships had gone down in the mouth of the harbor, blocking off the exit and entrance to the harbor. There was hope.

REBUILDING IN THE AFTERMATH

Immediately after the attack, men were hard at work trying to salvage and repair the ships that had been bombed. Using the dry docks and oil tanks that had been spared during the attack, repair efforts went faster than expected after such a horrific event.

The *Nevada*, the *West Virginia*, and the *California* were repaired and returned to duty, as were the *Tennessee*, the *Maryland*, and the *Pennsylvania*, which were back in action in less than two weeks. The *Oklahoma* was not repaired, but was brought up and righted. Five destroyed ships were stripped for usable parts.

Upon raising the *West Virginia* and hauling her into dry dock, repairmen discovered the bodies of 20 U.S. sailors who had been trapped inside awaiting rescue. Scratches made by the trapped men revealed that someone was still alive as late as December 23, more than two weeks after the ship went down.

The 1,760-pound (798-kg) bomb that ripped open the *Arizona* sealed the fate of 1,177 of the 1,511 crew members the morning of December 7, 1941. The ship was one of two that was left where it sank in the harbor. In the days following the attack, the U.S. Navy wanted to raise the ship to remove the bodies of the sailors. Medical examiners, however, advised that trying to exhume the bodies would be fruitless. Most of the men would have been burned so badly, it would be impossible to identify them. The men who lost their lives aboard the battleship were considered to be buried at sea in the bottom of the 40-foot (12-m) harbor.

The *Arizona* and the *Utah* were left where they had gone down. They later became memorials, but not until after the U.S. Navy had taken two triple gun turrets off the *Arizona* to use on another ship. The airfields were resurfaced and barracks and hangars were rebuilt.

Surrender

The Japanese surprise attack on Pearl Harbor may have been successful, but winning the battle did not mean Japan would win the war. The Imperial Japanese Navy controlled the Pacific for the first

The Japanese signed a formal surrender document
in Tokyo Bay on September 2, 1945.

six months after the attack. But the United States
was swift to rebuild and mounted a counterattack
in the Pacific that would crush the Japanese. The
Allied powers successfully waged war against the Axis
Alliance in the Atlantic and Pacific arenas.

By the time the Japanese surrendered on August
14, 1945—celebrated as VJ (Victory over Japan)
Day—the U.S. Navy had sunk every Japanese aircraft
carrier, battleship, and cruiser that had been part of
the strike force against Pearl Harbor. Triumphantly,

when Japan signed the surrender document on September 2, 1945, among the U.S. warships in Tokyo Bay was the USS *West Virginia*, which had been a victim of the surprise attack on Pearl Harbor nearly four years earlier.

USS *Arizona* Memorial

Beginning in 1943, survivors and veterans raised money for a memorial to the men of the *Arizona* who lost their lives. In 1958, President Dwight D. Eisenhower authorized the site as a national memorial. With federal funding and private donations, the USS *Arizona* Memorial was completed in 1961. The dedication occurred on Memorial Day 1962.

Designed by Alfred Preis, the memorial is a 184-foot (56-m) curved structure. It spans across the sunken *Arizona*, but does not touch any part of the ship. The flagpole is attached to the severed mainmast of the ship. The 21 large openings in the sides and roof of the white structure represent the 21-gun salute given to members of the military when they die.

Each year, thousands of people visit the memorial to pay tribute to those who lost their lives on December 7, 1941. The names of each of the 1,177 men who died are carved in a marble wall. All surviving *Arizona* crew members have the option to be interred in the memorial upon their deaths.

After more than 60 years, small drops of oil still leak from the ship and rise to the surface. Some say this represents the ship, still bleeding under the water. The USS *Arizona* has become a memorial to honor all military members killed on December 7, 1941.

The USS Arizona memorial in Pearl Harbor

TIMELINE

1931	1939	1940
Japanese forces invade Manchuria on September 18.	Germany invades Poland on September 1. World War II begins.	On September 27, Japan becomes part of the Axis Alliance with Germany and Italy.

1941	1941	1941
On December 7 at 3:42 a.m., a U.S. minesweeper, the *Condor,* spots a Japanese sub. The *Ward* searches for the sub.	On December 7 at 6:00 a.m., Japanese pilots begin takeoff from aircraft carriers more than 200 miles (300 km) north of Hawaii.	On December 7 at 6:45 a.m., the USS *Ward* sinks one of the midget submarines.

1941

1941

1941

In June, Japanese pilots begin to train for a possible air raid against the United States.

In October, Admiral Yamamoto receives approval to strike the U.S. Naval Fleet at Pearl Harbor.

On November 26, Japanese are en route to destroy the U.S. Naval Fleet at Pearl Harbor.

1941

1941

1941

On December 7 at 6:53 a.m., Lieutenant Outerbridge alerts Naval Headquarters of a sub in the area.

On December 7 at 7:02 a.m., army radar station operators see a large blip of planes quickly approaching Pearl Harbor.

On December 7 at 7:55 a.m., the first wave of Japanese bombers and fighters begin a surprise attack on Pearl Harbor.

TIMELINE

1941

On December 7 at 8:10 a.m., a bomb explodes on the forward deck of the *Arizona*, killing 1,177 men.

1941

On December 7 at 9:55 a.m., Japanese airplanes complete the second wave of the attack.

1941

On December 7 at 1:00 p.m., the Japanese special task force sets course to return to Japan.

1942

The president signs Executive Order 9066 on February 19. Japanese on the U.S. West Coast are relocated to internment camps.

1945

On August 14, Japan surrenders to the Allied powers.

1941

On December 8, President Roosevelt delivers his "Day of Infamy" speech, and Congress declares war on Japan.

1941

General Short and Admiral Kimmel are relieved of their commands on December 17.

1961

The USS *Arizona* Memorial is completed.

1988

U.S. Congress admits the injustice of the internment of Japanese civilians during World War II.

ESSENTIAL FACTS

DATE OF EVENT

December 7, 1941

PLACE OF EVENT

Pearl Harbor, Oahu, U.S. territory of Hawaii

KEY PLAYERS

❖ Emperor Hirohito, emperor of Japan

❖ Admiral Isoroku Yamamoto, commander of Japanese Combined Fleet

❖ Admiral Husband E. Kimmel, commander in chief of U.S. Pacific Fleet

❖ Lieutenant General Walter C. Short, commander, U.S. Army's Hawaiian Department

❖ Commander Mitsuo Fuchida, leader of Japanese strike force

❖ Franklin D. Roosevelt, president of the United States

Highlights of Event

The Imperial Japanese Navy attacked the U.S. Pacific Fleet at Pearl
Harbor, forcing the United States into World War II. The Japanese
strategically planned a surprise attack on a Sunday morning, just
before 8:00 a.m., catching U.S. military personnel unaware.

The goal of the Japanese strike force was to take out as many
U.S. ships and airplanes as possible to cripple the strength of the
U.S. Pacific Fleet. This would force the United States to accept a
negotiated peace settlement to recognize Japan's dominance in East
Asia.

In just two hours, the United States suffered massive loss of life and
damage to its fleet:

❖ 2,388 U.S. lives lost, including 48 civilians

❖ 1,178 wounded

❖ 2 battleships lost

❖ 19 sunken or damaged ships

❖ 164 aircraft destroyed

❖ 159 aircraft damaged

The Japanese lost 29 planes, 5 midget submarines, and less than
100 men.

Quote

"Yesterday, December 7, 1941—a date which will live in infamy—the
United States of America was suddenly and deliberately attacked
by naval and air forces of the Empire of Japan."—*President Franklin D.
Roosevelt, Monday, December 8, 1941*

ADDITIONAL RESOURCES

SELECT BIBLIOGRAPHY

Friedrich, Otto. "Day of Infamy." *Time Online*. 12 Nov. 2007 <http://www.time.com/time/magazine/article/ 0,9171,974391-1,00.html>.

Lord, Walter. *Day of Infamy*. New York: Henry Holt & Company, LLC, 1985.

Prange, Gordon W. *At Dawn We Slept: The Untold Story of Pearl Harbor.* New York: Penguin Books, 1982.

Prange, Gordon W. *December 7, 1941: The Day the Japanese Attacked Pearl Harbor.* New York: McGraw-Hill, 1988.

Shapiro, William E. *Pearl Harbor.* Turning Points of World War II Series. New York: Franklin Watts, a Grolier Company, 1984.

FURTHER READING

McGowan, Tom. *The Attack on Pearl Harbor.* Cornerstones of Freedom. Second Series: Children's Press. New York: Scholastic Inc., 2002.

McNeese, Tim. *The Attack on Pearl Harbor: America Enters World War II.* Greensboro, NC: Morgan Reynolds Publishers, 2002.

Pierce, Alan. *The Bombing of Pearl Harbor.* American Moments: ABDO & Daughters. Edina, MN: ABDO Publishing Company, 2005.

Van der Vat, Dan. *Pearl Harbor: The Day of Infamy—An Illustrated History.* Toronto, ON: The Madison Press Limited, 2001.

Web Links

To learn more about Pearl Harbor, visit ABDO Publishing Company online at **www.abdopublishing.com**. Web sites about Pearl Harbor are featured on our Book Links page. These links are routinely monitored and updated to provide the most current information available.

Places To Visit

USS *Arizona* Memorial
1 Arizona Memorial Place, Honolulu, HI 96818
808-422-2771
www.nps.gov/usar
The memorial, constructed over the site of the sunken USS *Arizona*, honors those who lost their lives on December 7, 1941.

USS *Arizona* Memorial Museum and Visitor Center
1 Arizona Memorial Place, Pearl Harbor, Honolulu, HI 96818
808-422-2771
www.arizonamemorial.org
The National Park Museum is filled with exhibits that contain letters, telegrams, and eyewitness photography of the attack on Pearl Harbor.

World War II Memorial
900 Ohio Drive, Southwest, Washington, DC 20024
202-426-6841
www.nps.gov/nwwm
The National World War II Memorial honors the men and women who sacrificed their lives during World War II and celebrates the victory of the United States over the Axis powers.

GLOSSARY

antiaircraft
A weapon designed to destroy hostile aircraft.

artillery
Large-caliber guns such as cannons and howitzers.

asphyxiate
Cause death by the lack of oxygen resulting in death.

assets
Property and resources.

attaché
A diplomat with special expert knowledge.

cartography
The science of making maps.

conning tower
A raised structure on a submarine's deck used for navigation.

cruiser
A heavily armed warship that is lighter, faster, and easier to maneuver than a battleship.

destroyer
A heavily armed warship that supports other ships in the fleet.

embargo
A legal prohibition on trade with a certain country.

enlist
To sign up for military service.

jettison
To throw items overboard.

list
To tilt to one side, especially a ship or boat.

magazine
A room that stores gunpowder and explosives.

minelayer
A naval vessel that deploys underwater mines.

minesweeper
A warship that removes or neutralizes mines.

port
The left side of a ship.

posthumously
After death.

reconnaissance
Preliminary military information gathering.

rendezvous
A meeting at a specific time and place.

sabotage
To destroy property.

shrapnel
Exploding shell fragments.

starboard
The right side of a ship.

strafe
The act of firing a machine gun from low-flying aircraft.

tarmac
A runway for airplanes.

torpedo
A self-propelled underwater explosive weapon.

yeoman
A member of the navy who performs clerical duties.

SOURCE NOTES

Chapter 1. December 6, 1941
1. Walter Lord. *Day of Infamy.* New York: Henry Holt & Company, LLC, 1985. 4.

Chapter 2. A World at War
1. "Lend-lease." *Encyclopedia Britannica 2007.* Encyclopedia Britannica Online Library Edition. 29 Dec. 2007 <http://www.library. eb.com/eb/article-9047741>.
2."Radio Address to the Democratic National Convention Accepting the Nomination." *The American Presidency Project.*
7 Apr. 2008 <http://www.presidency.ucsb.edu/ws/print. php?pid=15980>.

Chapter 3. Plans to Attack
1. "Bushido." *Encyclopedia Britannica 2007.* Encyclopedia Britannica Online Library Edition. 29 Dec. 2007 <http://www.library. eb.com/eb/article-9018271>.
2. Gordon W. Prange. *At Dawn We Slept: The Untold Story of Pearl Harbor.* New York: Penguin Books, 1982. 10.
3. Ibid. 16.
4. Ibid. 17.
5. Ibid. 16.
6. Ibid. 11.
7. Dan Van der Vat. *Pearl Harbor: The Day of Infamy—An Illustrated History.* Toronto, ON: Madison Press Books, 2001. 26.
8. Gordon W. Prange. *At Dawn We Slept: The Untold Story of Pearl Harbor.* New York: Penguin Books, 1982. 445.
9. Ibid. 445.

Chapter 4. Into the War
1. Walter Lord. *Day of Infamy.* New York: Henry Holt & Company, LLC, 1985. 29.
2. Ibid. 35.
3. Ibid. 28.
4. Ibid. 39.
5. Ibid. 44.
6. Ibid. 45.
7. Ibid.

8. George E. Elliott Jr. "There's Nothing Wrong with Our Radar!" *Pearl Harbor.com*. 29 Dec. 2007 <http://www.pearl-harbor.com/georgeelliott/index.html>.

Chapter 5. *Tora! Tora! Tora!*
1. Gordon W. Prange. *At Dawn We Slept: The Untold Story of Pearl Harbor.* New York: Penguin Books, 1982. 502.
2. Gordon W. Prange. *December 7, 1941: The Day the Japanese Attacked Pearl Harbor.* New York: McGraw-Hill, 1988. 109.
3. Gordon W. Prange. *At Dawn We Slept: The Untold Story of Pearl Harbor.* New York: Penguin Books, 1982. 504.
4. Ibid. 503.

Chapter 6. The First Wave Strikes
1. Gordon W. Prange. *At Dawn We Slept: The Untold Story of Pearl Harbor.* New York: Penguin Books, 1982. 506.
2. Ibid.
3. Ibid. 517.
4. Ibid. 509.
5. Ibid. 513.
6. Dan Van der Vat. *Pearl Harbor: The Day of Infamy—An Illustrated History.* Toronto, ON: Madison Press Books, 2001. 103.
7. Ibid. 106.

Chapter 7. Terror Continues on Battleship Row
1. Gordon W. Prange. *At Dawn We Slept: The Untold Story of Pearl Harbor.* New York: Penguin Books, 1982. 507.
2. Ibid.
3. Ibid.
4. Otto Friedrich. "Day of Infamy." *Time Online.* 12 Nov. 2007 <http://www.time.com/time/magazine/article/0,9171,974391-1,00.html>.
5. Naval Historical Center. 28 Nov. 2007 <http://www.history.navy.mil/faqs/faq57-4.htm>.
6. Ibid.
7. "U.S.S. Arizona BB-39 and Pearl Harbor Remembrance Page." *USS Arizona.org.* 31 Dec. 2007 < http://www.ussarizona.org/survivors/carson/index.html>.

Source Notes Continued

Chapter 8. Airfields under Attack
1. Walter Lord. *Day of Infamy.* New York: Henry Holt & Company, LLC, 1985. 80.
2. Gordon W. Prange. *At Dawn We Slept: The Untold Story of Pearl Harbor.* New York: Penguin Books, 1982. 519.
3. Ibid. 523.
4. Dan Van der Vat. *Pearl Harbor: The Day of Infamy — An Illustrated History.* Toronto, ON: Madison Press Books, 2001. 127.
5. Gordon W. Prange. *At Dawn We Slept: The Untold Story of Pearl Harbor.* New York: Penguin Books, 1982. 534.
6. Ibid. 125.

Chapter 9. Second Wave of Attacks
1. "Historical Documents." *The Children of the Camps Project.* 30 Dec. 2007 <http://www.children-of-the-camps.org/history/civilact.html>.
2. Gordon W. Prange. *At Dawn We Slept: The Untold Story of Pearl Harbor.* New York: Penguin Books, 1982. 563.
3. "A Pearl Harbor Survivor's Story." *SouthernUtah.com.* 31 Dec. 2007 <http://historytogo.utah.gov/utah_chapters/from_war_to_war/utahnsurvivestheattackatpearlharbor.html>.

Chapter 10. A Nation Responds
1. *Pearl Harbor.org.* 27 Nov. 2007 <http://www.pearlharbor.org/speech-fdr-infamy-1941.asp>.
2. "Beyond the Movie: Pearl Harbor." *National Geographic.* 31 Dec. 2007 <http://plasma.nationalgeographic.com/pearlharbor/ngbeyond/people/people7.html>.

INDEX

INDEX CONTINUED

ABOUT THE AUTHOR

Susan E. Hamen is a full-time editor who finds her most rewarding career experiences to be writing and editing children's books. Hamen lives in Minnesota with her family. In her spare time, she enjoys reading, traveling, and camping. She dedicates this book to her husband Ryan, for his steadfast support of all of her endeavors, and to her brother David, whose passion for studying all things related to World War II is inspiring.

PHOTO CREDITS

AP Images, cover, 13, 14, 21, 29, 30, 41, 42, 44, 47, 50, 53, 59, 60, 75, 77, 78, 81, 86, 93; Philip Coblentz/Jupiterimages/AP Images, 6; Keystone/Stringer/Getty Images, 22, 32; Ernest K. Bennett/AP Images, 49; Three Lions/Stringer/Getty Images, 63, 85; Hulton Archive/Stringer/Getty Images, 67; Time Life Pictures/Stringer/Getty Images, 68; Jack Fields/Corbis, 95